THE ADVENTURES OF SKEETER AND THENA

THE CASE OF THE CURIOUS RAT

By

Benjamin Grady

"The Adventures of Skeeter & Thena:

The Case of the Curious Rat"

Copyright © Benjamin Joseph Grady 2014

All Rights Reserved. Without limiting the rights under copyright reserved above, no part of this publication may be reproduced, stored in or introduced into a retrieval system in any form or by any means (electronic, mechanical, photocopying, recording or otherwise) without the written permission of the author of this book.

ISBN: 978-1-7364407-0-4

Table of Contents

Chapter One---Escape Artist	1
Chapter Two---The Lazy Lizard	9
Chapter Three---She's Out of Here	18
Chapter Four---Where's the Beef	29
Chapter Five---That Darn Rat!	37
Chapter Six---A new Friend	46
Chapter Seven---A tunnel to Nowhere	65
Chapter Eight---Run Away Home	83
Chapter Nine---Ride 'em Cowboy	94
Acknowledgments	115

Chapter One

Escape Artist

Skeeter slowly rose from the soft wood shavings she had buried herself under when she heard the soft birdsong drifting in from the window. Tiny bits of the soft shavings stuck to her gray fur, and she rose to stretch the sleep from her legs while gently scratching behind her ear at a shred of wood that had gotten stuck there.

Skeeter remembered how much she loved and treasured this time of year, as she basked in the early sunrises that gave her more time to enjoy the beautiful bird songs and enjoy their melodies.

High-pitched whistles rang out through the morning air, and drifted through the open window as Skeeter sauntered over to the small yellow and red bowl that held her breakfast. She quickly scarfed down the few remaining scraps of the small dried fruits, and then washed her meal down with a few sips from the water bottle hanging on one side of her cage. She loved the small dried fruits the most, so she always ate them first from her morning breakfast mix. The absolute best part had to be the purple yogurt balls! They were only mixed in occasionally, but Skeeter was always sure to stash those away in her tunnel immediately.

After her belly felt full, Skeeter promptly began her morning cleaning ritual. She started with her nose and whiskers then licked her paws and rubbed them over her face to remove any grit from her long night's sleep. Before she got to the ear-cleaning part of her ritual, the black music box thingy on the night stand next to the bed began to screech and blast loud music!

Skeeter peered outside her cage, and watched the figure under the pink and white blanket roll around for a while before finally sitting up on the edge of the bed. A slender hand darted out from the blanket, and firmly slapped the top of the black music box thingy that blared noisily every morning at the same time. Skeeter watched as the young girl quickly dressed herself, pulling on a pair of blue jeans and a pink hooded sweat shirt before she started brushing her long, blond hair in front of the tall mirror. Skeeter loved to watch Amyah brush her long, blond curls until they were shiny, soft and bouncy.

Of all the humans Skeeter knew, Amyah was definitely her absolute favorite! Amyah was always extremely kind and caring, and she had an innocence and sweetness to her that no other human could fake. Skeeter loved to burrow in to Amyah's long blond hair, as it was always so warm and cozy. The rest of the family was great too, but Skeeter felt a special connection with the curly-haired girl that started the day they met. Shivers crept up Skeeter's spine when she thought back to that day, and how close Skeeter had come to being snake food.

The first home Skeeter lived in had been nice—at first. She lived in a large glass tank with dozens of other rats, where they played games all day and slept in small cozy piles at night. Every few days a woman would come and take one of their older friends away, and all the rats would get sad. The younger rats didn't know where the woman would take their older friends, but since they never came back the young ones just imagined that their friends were taken to some other wonderful place where older rats would play games and have fun. The young rats would miss their older friends and be sad for a while, but eventually life would return to normal. New rats would be born, with their pink hairless skin and eyes closed tight as if afraid of the light. The baby rats would grow older, and the older rats would be taken away by the woman. It was just the way things were.

The rats never knew the woman's name because she only appeared long enough to feed them and take another friend away. Other than that, it had been a good life in the cage. Until the fateful day the woman came to take Skeeter away! Skeeter figured it was just her turn to leave the tank, and she looked forward to seeing all those old friends that had been taken before her. Skeeter hadn't been the least bit scared until she found herself dangling by her tail; head first, over another tank with the biggest, ugliest, most vicious looking monster she had ever seen! The hideous creature was staring back at Skeeter, hungrily flipping and flicking its tongue out to taste the air! In that instant, an all-consuming fear filled Skeeter's body, and she lost control over all her legs. Within seconds, Skeeter found her strength and began flailing her legs, clawing at the woman's hand with her back feet, in a futile attempt to escape. The woman never flinched, and held tightly to Skeeter's tail despite her frantic clawing. In that moment, escape seemed impossible, and Skeeter instantly knew her life had come to an end.

"Nooooooo!" Skeeter heard an ear-splitting scream from an unfamiliar voice that echoed around the room. "What are you doing to that poor thing?!" The voice belonged to Amyah, and she repeated her question as she marched through the doorway.

"I'm feeding Zeus, my snake. Why?" The woman was visibly annoyed at the little girl, and continued to dangle Skeeter over the tank.

"Oh no, you're not," Amyah said, in an authoritative tone. "I just can't believe you're going to feed that poor little innocent creature to your mean old snake! How dare you!"

"Amyah, sweetheart, my snake has to eat too." Skeeter just couldn't believe how the large woman talked about feeding her to the snake like it was no big deal! Terror gripped Skeeter's heart as she thought about all the other rats the woman had taken from the tank. Had this been their fate also? Had the woman fed them to this hideous creature, as he sat coiled up and fat while looking smugly at Skeeter from the bottom of this tank? Skeeter wanted to burst into tears when she thought about all the friends she lost to this evil woman and her creepy monster snake.

"Well, he's not going to eat THAT rat," Amyah said in a matter-of-fact voice, shaking her curly-haired head with her hands on her hips in defiance.

"What do you want me to do Amyah? Let my snake die?" The woman looked so smug and sure Amyah would back down, and she let out a boisterous laugh at Amyah. Skeeter thought a dead snake sounded like the most wonderful idea ever!

Skeeter still remembered the comforting feeling that washed over her when Amyah marched over to the woman, snatched Skeeter from the woman's grip, then gently cradled Skeeter on her shoulder. Skeeter was surprised at how safe she felt in the little girl's hands that day, and they were inseparable ever since!

Amyah did everything with Skeeter! She danced, listened to music, did homework, and talked on the phone; all with Skeeter perched on her shoulder, burrowing underneath Amyah's long, golden hair. Sometimes Amyah would even fall asleep on accident in her large comfy bed with Skeeter still hidden in her long locks. Skeeter loved those nights the most because she could snuggle into the soft pillows, breathe in the scent of the little girl, and listen to the slow, rhythmic, and comforting sound of Amyah's heartbeat.

"I'll see you later Skeeter," Amyah said, and that drew Skeeter's thoughts back to the present.

Skeeter responded with a series of squeaks she knew the human girl couldn't understand, but, as always, it still brought a smile to Amyah's face. She loved that smile, framed by those beautiful, shiny blond curls. Skeeter hated when the girl had to leave for whatever that place called school was, but for some reason the girl's parents said she had to go. Skeeter sadly watched Amyah leave through the decorated doorway of her room, as she swiftly knelt to grab her book bag along the way while yelling at her brother Max to hurry or they would be late for school.

Skeeter finished grooming herself while hoping and waiting to see if Amyah return for something she may have forgotten. She continued grooming her ears, worked her way down to her hind legs, and then finished up her morning ritual by cleaning her tail. Once enough time passed without any sign of Amyah's return, Skeeter set to work on the cage door's latch. Within seconds, the door swung open and Skeeter was free to roam the open space of the UPSTAIRS!

Chapter Two

The Lazy Lizard

Thena lounged lazily on her basking rock, absorbing the heat and light that shone from the lamps above her tank. Her legs were spread out to her sides, and it looked as if she was hugging the fake stone, gripping it with her long, needle-thin claws. The spikes on Thena's head and sides stuck out like the thorns on a rose, and her soft belly bulged from her recent feast of crickets and meal worms. Thena loved being a bearded dragon, and just couldn't imagine life as anything else!

Basking under the heat lamps was her favorite activity, other than playing with her boy Max. Recently, Thena got very little time to play with Max because he spent less time with her as he grew older. Thena knew Max still loved her, but she longed for the days when she had been a young dragon, crawling all over the house with Max trailing behind on his hands and knees trying to keep up. The thing she missed most was the long hours she spent lying on his chest, listening to the slow, rhythmic pounding of his heart as he read. It made her feel connected to the boy in ways she had never felt before. It was a deep connection that only the noblest of lizards, a bearded dragon, could feel with a human boy.

Thena tilted her head in aggravation as a cricket chirped in the corner. She hated when she missed one of the little bugs because they an annoyance with their constant chirping, and it also meant her hunting skills weren't up to bearded dragon standards. Thena decided she would have to work on that. It just wouldn't do to have anyone see her lax on her hunting skills. After some thought, Thena finally decided not to waste excess energy hunting the cricket and left the annoying little bug for later, maybe as an evening snack.

The Box that showed pictures and made sounds turned itself on, which signaled that Max would be getting up soon. He always waited until the last few minutes to get up, so it was always comical to watch the boy pull on his clothes in a hurry, then gather up his things in a rush as he bolted down the stairs. But Thena hoped this day would be different. After a few minutes, the boy started to show some signs of life underneath his Star Wars comforter. Thena grew hopeful, thinking that maybe he would make time for her this morning. But as more time passed without Max getting out of bed, Thena slowly came to realize that quality time with Max would surely not happen that morning.

"Max! What are you doing?" Amyah marched into Max's room, demanding an answer. "Get up now or you're going to miss the bus again!"

"Ok, ok," Max grumbled sleepily. "I'm up." Max slowly rose and pushed his legs from under the covers, still rubbing the sleep from his eyes while sitting on the edge of the bed.

Amyah shook her head at Max's slow, snail-like movements. "It amazes me that you even manage to get to school, sleepy head," she said. "You stayed up late playing video games again, didn't you?"

"Nope," Max lied. "I stayed up late doing homework."

Thena wasn't one to tattletale, but she had been awake, sleeplessly, for half the night because of the loud shooting and explosions coming from the box that the kids called a TV. Max had been glued to the TV for the better part of the evening. By the look on his younger sister's face, Thena could tell that Amyah didn't believe Max's "homework" story either. And rightly so.

"Don't give me that look." Max rolled his eyes at Amyah, and sighed heavily. "Wait until you get into high school. Then you'll understand," he warned.

"Oh, I'm sure you have LOTS of homework in high school," Amyah replied sarcastically. "I just don't believe that you stayed up late doing it last night," she said with a smirk.

"Whatever…," said Max, pulling his shirt over his head to muffle his colorful rebuttal.

"Ok. See you down stairs. And hurry up!" Amyah cut Max off, mid-grumble, and headed down the stairs from Max's room to the first floor with her blond curls bouncing behind her.

Thena liked the younger sister. Not as much as her boy Max, but there was a kindness in her eyes that Thena didn't see in too many humans. A kindness that made you feel safe, and that made you feel like you always had a place in her life. She was also very funny and had a deep love for all animals. Amyah was notorious for bringing home any stray animal she could find, no matter how many times her parents told her not to. So far, she had rescued and found homes for three cats, a litter of kittens, a dog, a box of baby bunnies, four turtles, two birds and a squirrel! All rescued and nursed back to health with Amyah's love and attention. Amyah was a rare gem among the humans that Thena hoped would never change. Unlike Max, who was a good boy, although he spent less and less time with Thena as he got older.

Max stood in front of the mirror, and then ran his fingers through his hair a few times before finally shrugging his shoulders and disappearing down the stairs. It made Thena laugh to think about just how careless the boy had become with his appearance! He wasn't dirty or smelly or anything like that, though. Thena just noticed that he just didn't spend a lot of time on things like combing his hair anymore, and Thena knew all too well the value humans placed on things like combing their hair!

"Hey, Thena! How's it going today? Good? I'm good. I know she just left, but I already can't wait for Amyah to get home so we can have some fun…." Thena almost had trouble keeping up with Skeeter and her rapid-fire fast way of speaking. The way the rat talked made Thena think of a woodpecker, determined to get his lunch from the bark of a tree. Tap-tap-tap-tap-tap…. Skeeter's chatter was a non-stop, rapid rhythm, on and on! The rat could talk so fast it appeared that she never even took a breath between sentences!

"….and she said she would be right home after school. Do you think she will be right home? I hope she…" Skeeter continued, until Thena cut her off, mid-sentence.

"Skeeter, relax. If she said she would be home, then I'm sure she will be." Thena finally managed to get a word in! A rarity!

Skeeter tilted her head, and then stood up on her hind legs as if she smelled something in the air, before finally saying, "I suppose you're right."

Skeeter circled around to the front of Thena's tank to where the two wires for the heat lamps hung down. Skeeter used the wires for traction, and started climbing up to the top of the tank. Thena watched as the small grey rat scampered up the black wire, her long hairless tail flipping about. Once again, Thena admired the skill it took for Skeeter to climb a wire no bigger than her own leg.

Ever since Skeeter had figured out the door on her cage didn't lock properly, this had been their morning ritual. The children would leave for school, and then Skeeter would climb on top of Thena's tank and spend the better part of the day trying to convince Thena that they could let her out of the large glass aquarium if they thought hard enough about it. Thena didn't have the heart to tell Skeeter that she didn't really want to get out. Since it made the rat happy to think up various means to help Thena escape the aquarium, and it kept her busy (which meant she wasn't bothering Thena with rapid fire questions), Thena saw the morning ritual as a win for both of them.

"Now, back to what I was saying yesterday. I think if we could get this door open, the hinges would allow it to swing inward. Then you could climb up that fake stone thingy, jump up to the door, and then climb out." Skeeter had made her way to the top of the tank and was standing on the metal grating that covered it.

"First of all," Thena began in her best lecturing voice, "it's not a 'thingy.' It's a fake tree stump. Let's at least try not to use the word 'thingy.' Secondly, there is no way that I would be able to make that jump. Rats may be good jumpers, but jumping definitely isn't what bearded dragons do best."

"Oh reeeeally? I thought beardies were good at everything," Skeeter said mockingly. "I'm going to have to remember that the next time you start lecturing me on your hunting skills."

"Oh, stop! You and I both know what magnificent hunters dragons are. There is no need for us to even discuss it." Thena was becoming incensed.

"Well…I don't know any other birdies to compare your hunting skills to, so I really couldn't say…" Skeeter began, needling Thena just to aggravate her. However, Skeeter paused when she saw the skin under Thena's chin start to bulge like a bullfrog's. The bulging chin is one way that dragons revealed their emotions, and it was how they came to be called bearded dragons. The skin stretched until it was about the size of a large marble, and then it started to turn faintly black. This display was meant as a warning to other animals who dared to cross a bearded dragon. Skeeter, all too familiar with her beardy friend, knew when it was time to shut up. Skeeter quickly switched to busily working on the latch of the gate.

Thena quietly laughed to herself. She hated to make Skeeter think that she was angry, but sometimes it was the only way to get a little peace and quiet.

Chapter Three

She's Out of Here

Skeeter worked on the latch for a bit before deciding that it was a lost cause. She sat back on her hind legs and closely examined it a bit more. The latch had a metal loop thingy that worked just like the gate on her cage, so she knew if she could apply enough pressure, it would spring open. Skeeter also thought that if she was sitting on the gate when it opened, it would actually swing down into the tank instead of out. The only problem was that this latch was made of a stronger metal then her own cage latch, so Skeeter would somehow need to apply a lot more pressure. Skeeter thought about all the little tricks she had come up for her latch since she moved in with Amyah and tried applying them to the latch, with no success.

Skeeter's own cage had been easy enough to break out of after a couple of failed attempts. Now, Skeeter had her cage door rigged so it looked closed all the way, but still allowed Skeeter to move freely. She surveyed Max's room to see if she could find something useful. Against one wall was Max's bed, decorated with characters from his favorite movie –Star Wars. The other wall had a low chest of drawers with a large television that Max spent endless amounts of time watching and playing games on. As typical of Max's room, the rest of the room had bits of odds and ends lying all around. There were magazines and half-read books strewn about, a small pile of clothes in one corner, and a collection of shoes spilling out of his closet. Seeing the collection of shoes gave Skeeter a brilliant idea.

Skeeter scurried down the wires and ran across the room to the pile of shoes. Max was notorious for just kicking his shoes off into a pile outside his closet, no matter how many times his mother told him not to do it. Skeeter quietly thanked him for doing so as she made her way across the bumpy carpet. She made her way to the pile of shoes and started pulling the shoelace of a black and white running shoe through the holes. It got more difficult as she made her way toward the toe of the shoe, but the white shoelace eventually passed freely though the last hole. With a squeak of triumph, Skeeter rapidly made her way back across the room holding the shoelace between her teeth, the ends dangling behind her and occasionally getting tangled up in her back feet as she trotted back toward Thena's glass tank.

The tricky part was going to be convincing Thena to help her, but Skeeter knew that if she could run the ends of the shoelace down into the tank, then loop the middle around the latch, Thena would be able to jump up, grab the shoelace ends, use her weight to pull the latch free, and the door would swing open. Skeeter quietly congratulated herself on coming up with such a wonderful, clever plan. Only the smartest of rats could have ever come up with such an ingenious idea, and there was clearly no way some smarty-pants bearded dragon could ever think of doing such a thing.

As soon as Skeeter climbed back up the lamp wires to the top of the cage, she set about her work. First, she looped the middle of the shoelace around the latch. Then, Skeeter slowly fed the ends of the shoelace down into the tank, and then looked at Thena.

Thena looked up at Skeeter with her head cocked to one side, like she always did every time Skeeter was up to something Thena might not approve.

Sensing Thena's puzzlement, Skeeter said, "Now, you just have to jump up and grab the ends of the shoelace with your mouth, and your weight will pull it open."

Thena squinted one eye, and stared up at Skeeter as if waiting for Skeeter to laugh at some hilarious joke. "You have got to be kidding me!" Thena was clearly not amused. "This is your grand plan?"

"It's the perfect plan. It'll work. You'll see." Skeeter was supremely confident in her plan.

"Aggg, just leave me alone, please." Thena was beginning to get impatient. "I've got more important things to do right now than listen to silly ideas from a silly little rat." Thena circled her basking rock a few times, with her belly rubbing the surface to test the temperature before she stretched out on the rock again to soak up the heat from the overhead lamps.

Skeeter was starting to get aggravated with the stubborn lizard, but knew if she let her aggravation show that Thena would only dig in her heels harder and refuse to cooperate. Then the gate would never get open.

Skeeter quickly decided that begging wasn't working on the stubborn beardy, so she put on the most innocent of faces she could think of for her next strategy.

"Thena, I promise that if you try this one little thing, I will never, ever bother you again about getting out."

Thena's eyes flipped open almost instantly at this new suggestion, and Thena slowly craned her neck around to look directly into Skeeter's eyes.

Skeeter tried to stifle her giggles as they rose in her throat because she knew there was no way the lizard would pass up an offer like that. Skeeter and Thena locked eyes for what felt like an eternity before the lizard decided to speak.

Thena hesitated a bit at first, and then slowly asked, "What about when the kids get home and they see that the gate is open?"

"Oh, they'll just think it came open by itself, or that they forgot to close it when they left," Skeeter replied just as carefully. "Besides, it may not even work and then you can go on with the rest of your day without having to hear another word from me."

"Not just the rest of the day," Thena quickly added, "you said that I would never have to hear another word about getting out of here again, ever."

"I know what I said and I promise. If you try this one thing I'll never ask you again, and I always keep my promises, you know that." Skeeter could see the thoughts racing behind Thena's eyes as she looked up at her. This was a big decision for the beardy, but Skeeter knew there was no way Thena would pass on an offer like this. If there was one thing Thena valued over anything else it was peace and quiet.

"Ok," was all the grumpy lizard said in reply.

Skeeter never saw Thena do anything but lie under her basking lights and hunt for crickets, which didn't take much energy. But Skeeter almost fell of the top of the aquarium when the large lizard suddenly sprang up from her hind legs, grabbed the two ends of the lace with her jaws, hung suspended in the air for a second, then landed softly on all fours when the gate sprang inward. It had been more than Skeeter could believe to see Thena leap so gracefully! Skeeter never knew the old lizard had it in her!

"That was amazing, Thena! How come you…"

Thena cut Skeeter off, mid-admiration. "Don't worry about it. Now remember your word and leave me alone."

"Yeah, but the gate is open now, so all you have to do…" Skeeter started to plead.

"Please, just leave me alone Skeeter. You promised me," Thena said.

"No, I actually promised never to bother you again with getting the gate open. It's open now, so jump on the door and climb up, and we'll go explore downstairs." Skeeter knew that going down stairs would bring on new protests, but she figured she might as well let Thena in on her little plan.

"Oh no, we don't go downstairs. So forget about exploring." Thena was serious.

"Haven't you ever wanted to see what was down there?" Skeeter asked. "How have you been here, in this cage, all these years and not once wanted to see what's down there?" Skeeter just couldn't believe that neither of them had been downstairs before, and that made her want to go exploring even more.

"I don't really care what's down there." Thena was not interested. "I, for one, am happy right where I am."

"Are you afraid?" Skeeter didn't really believe that Thena was afraid. She was just trying to motivate Thena into leaving her glass bubble.

"Don't go there, you little pest." Skeeter could tell that Thena was starting to get upset, so she decided she might as well take this all the way. "Oh, come on, Thena! Just jump up. It isn't that far."

"I don't feel like it, now leave me alone. It's bad enough that the door to my tank is now open. I can only imagine what the kids will think when they get home." Thena was so tired of Skeeter's pestering.

"Well, I'm going downstairs." Skeeter was ready to explore. "If you want to join me you can. If not, you can stay here and be your same old boring self."

"I'm telling you we can't go down stairs." Thena was serious. "What if someone comes home? We won't know it until it's too late, and don't you think they'll wonder how we got out of our cages?"

"We both know they'll be gone all day. The kids are at school and the parents are at work. We're all clear for at least half a day." Skeeter had already made up her mind that she was going downstairs. With or without Thena, she was going exploring. "I'm going!"

Skeeter quickly scaled down the black wires and was running across the floor before Thena could make another objection. She could barely make out a muffled voice from inside the glass tank by the time Skeeter made it to the top of the stairs. How many times had she stood in this very spot, looking down these stairs, wondering what excitement and adventure was at the bottom of them?

The hardwood stairs went down five steps, then turned left. Skeeter couldn't see what was beyond that left turn, but visions of new and exciting things raced through her mind.

For the short time Skeeter had been a part of the family, there had always been many different sounds and smells spiraling up those stairs to her cage. Now, Skeeter was finally going to see what was down there! She carefully crawled down the steps backward and took her time so she wouldn't hurt herself, especially since the hardwood was slippery under her padded feet. With each purposeful step, images of large wheels of cheese, huge containers of peanut butter, and endless bags of candy danced through her mind. Oh, how she loved candy! Not that Amyah would give her any, but occasionally the girl would leave some lying about and Skeeter would snatch it and hide it away. Skeeter imagined the long tunnel in her cage stocked full of candy of all different types.

The soft ones, the hard ones, even the ones that never seemed to get any smaller no matter how many times she licked on it. Skeeter slid down to the fifth step and took a peek to see what awaited her around the corner.

From this viewpoint, Skeeter couldn't see much other than another six steps that ended at a long hardwood hallway, a white door to the left, and an arched opening to the right were the floor changed to some kind of shiny surface made of large tiles. At the end of the hall, Skeeter could see there was another room with a hardwood floor, but she couldn't see much more beyond a small table with a lamp, and an exotic-looking huge potted plant. Skeeter couldn't contain her excitement any longer! Longing for something new, Skeeter threw caution to the wind, and raced head-long down the stairs to her destination!

Chapter Four

Where's the Beef?

Skeeter squeezed through the small opening she managed to create by pushing the cabinet door open with her nose. The dark interior smelled acidic and musky, and she could make out the outlines of large bottles with giant lettering, with smaller squirt bottles half-full of clear liquids. There was even some sort of short white handle with large blue feathers sticking out of one end. Skeeter thought the blue feathers would make a great place to cuddle up to, but it smelled heavy with dust and made her sneeze when she got too close so she stayed clear of it. After a few minutes looking around with only the dim light of the cracked cabinet to see by, she decided that there was nothing good in it, just like all the other ones she had explored. Her adventure thus far was quickly becoming a bust.

She couldn't believe that downstairs was just as boring as upstairs; where where the gigantic bags of candy and goodies that she always pictured being down here? Skeeter knew they had to be hidden somewhere down here because every time one of the children came up the stairs they would have something new to eat. She looked everywhere for the fluffy cotton candy, the sweet Jolly Ranchers, the gooey Laffy Taffy, and the amazing chocolate peanut butter cups. She searched high and low for those wonderful bags of chips: the salty ones with all the ridges and the cheesy ones that left orange stuff all over your paws when you ate them.

The living room was the first place Skeeter explored. It had a large brown couch with big fluffy cushions made out of some sort of soft, shiny material. She couldn't believe how wonderfully cool and soft the couch was underneath her paws, and she had even found a couple of tiny, soft, and chewy crumbs underneath a couple of the cushions to top it off! A large cabinet stood against one wall with the biggest TV Skeeter had ever seen in the middle of it. Somebody must have left on by accident when they left. Some humans with different colored t-shirts were racing across some logs that were tied together and floating on a lake. Skeeter was never surprised at the things humans would put themselves through for entertainment. A woman in a red t-shirt slipped while running across, sending her flailing, head-first into the dark water! It was so funny that Skeeter couldn't imagine anyone not laughing at it.

After exploring the living room, Skeeter crept along the back wall behind a small table holding a lamp and a black and white photo of what looked like the family when the two kids were a couple years younger. She accidentally bumped into one of the back legs of the table and it wobbled like it was ready to fall off! She backed against the wall for a minute, just in case it did decide to crash to the floor. After a second of wobbling back and forth, the leg finally stilled. She would have to be careful if she ever scampered behind the table again, and be extra-careful so she wouldn't have to find out if the whole table would come crashing down with the loss of the one leg.

The next room Skeeter explored was what seemed to be the parents' room. There was short grey carpeting, and a fireplace on one wall that must have been fake since it had a bright flame that looked real enough but Skeeter felt only glass and no heat when she tried to put a paw in the flame. There was a huge wooden dresser on the other wall, with a mirror on top that was just as large as the dresser. In the center of the room, Skeeter spied what had to be the biggest, fluffiest bed she had ever seen! The comforter was dark red with light brown squares stitched into it, and the pillows looked almost as big as the cushions on the couch and twice as fluffy. She couldn't imagine why the parents would need such a big bed to sleep in. Sure, the dad was a big guy, but not that big. She decided that it had to be one of the biggest beds that humans could make, and that more than two people must sleep in it. Maybe the kids would fall asleep there when they had family night, watching movies and laughing into the night.

After a quick search of the parents' room, Skeeter crossed the hall and finally made it to the room that she had been looking for the whole time. Ah, the kitchen, the room Skeeter had dreamed of since she shared her first bowl of Ramen Noodle soup, snatched her first slice of pepperoni pizza, and crunched on her first piece of candy! A room that was just down the stairs, yet still so far away. The dream seemed so much better than the reality as she scanned the room again for anything that might be edible.

Skeeter smelled food somewhere in this room; in fact, the whole room smelled of food, but she just couldn't find it! The strongest of the smells was vanilla mixed with cinnamon and some sort of fruit that she had never smelled before. There was also the smell of freshly cut flowers wafting from the round glass table in the middle of the kitchen. There was a good chance that all of the food was hidden high up in those cabinets above the long counter, but so far she hadn't found a way up to them or into that large silver box thingy that felt cool when she put her paw on it. She eyeballed the tall silver box one more time before deciding that it was going to be too much trouble.

"Why does this have to be so complicated?" Skeeter's voice echoed off the walls. She couldn't go back upstairs empty handed or else Thena would not only yell at her for going down the stairs, but also wouldn't believe she had gone all the way down if she didn't return with some evidence.

Skeeter heard a small sound that drew her attention. It was a white door with a window in the middle of it that had a clear view of the bright blue sky. At the bottom was a small opening with a flap moving back and forth in the breeze. Skeeter quickly hid behind the leg of a chair just in case something tried making its way into the opening, but after a few minutes of sniffing the air she decided it was all clear. She was making her way towards the white door when she realized it must be a door to the outside. Her heart beat faster at the thought of going outside! Why would the family have a door that small to the outside? Skeeter vaguely remembered Thena talking about how the family had once had a dog, and decided it must have been for the dog. She didn't think long on the question before she squired over to the small door, where a gust of wind rattled the flap once more and the smell of fresh air wafted into the room. It does go outside! Skeeter was so excited that she ran the rest of the way towards the white door and its flap, not wanting to waste any more time. She jumped up into the opening and squirmed under the flap. It was a tight fit and the stiff flap kept pushing her back inside, but Skeeter finally made it through the opening on her third attempt. Once outside, she jumped down onto a small set of hard grey stairs that felt warm from the mid-day sun and found herself under the bright sunlight and fresh air of a summer's day!

Skeeter made her way down the hard stairs into the cool green grass. It was refreshing, feeling the grass caress her furry sides and belly, and it felt wonderful compared to the wood shavings that she was used to feeling in her cage. The grass was tall, soft, and hugged the sides of her body as she rolled around in it and scraped her padded feet across the dirt while letting her short claws dig slightly into the earth. It was the most wonderful feeling Skeeter had in her short life. She wished that she could somehow talk Amyah into putting grass into her cage as she continued to roll around in its softness.

"Skeeter, watch out!" Skeeter flipped upright, and turned to see Thena standing just outside the white door.

Skeeter smiled at the worried looking lizard and knew that the yelling was going to start early. "Hey…" she started to say, but movement out of the corner of her eye caught her attention. Before Skeeter turned to look, a large shadow fell across her path as a sudden gust of wind and grass raised dust that stung her eyes. Soon, she felt an iron grip take hold of her around her middle, crushing the air from her lungs. Skeeter's body went limp as her eyes fought to stay open. The last thing the small rat remembered before she blacked out was the sight of the ground rushing away from her at an incredible speed.

Chapter Five

That Darn Rat!

Thena stared wide-eyed when Skeeter disappeared down the stairs, but Thena was even more surprised when she saw the small rat actually climbing through the small doggie door. It had aggravated Thena to no end that she had to climb out of her nice, warm tank and chase Skeeter, much less follow her down the stairs. Stairs might have been easy for rats to negotiate, but it wasn't the same for bearded dragons. Thena's claws scraping along the finished hardwood made her feel like she was trying to crawl on ice. No matter how fast she moved her legs they never seemed to get her very far. And trying to stop, well, that was something else entirely. All Thena had managed to do consistently well was bump her head on the walls while slipping and sliding the whole way down the stairs.

For the short time that Skeeter had been a part of the family, she had often stared down the stairs with that adventurous look in her eyes but always listened to reason and turned back. Thena didn't have the heart to tell her that there wasn't much down there. She liked that the rat thought there was some adventure somewhere in the house, but Thena knew that all the adventure disappeared when the kids had gotten older. Thena often thought of the old days when Max would carry her around the house on his shoulder and let her spend time chasing Ebony, the family's furry black dog.

Thena watched the flap on the doggie door as the last bit of Skeeter's tail disappeared behind it. What on earth would have made the rat go outside? Thena looked around the kitchen for any signs of the family. She didn't see any so she made her way to the white door, not sliding as much on the kitchen tiles as she did on the floors in the rest of the house.

That pesky, bawled-tailed vermin has a lot of explaining to do, Thena thought.

The kitchen always seemed so cold to Thena with its silver refrigerator, oven and that machine that washed the cups and bowls. Even the smallest of sounds seemed to echo off the walls, announcing her presence. The tiles felt cold under her feet, especially when the days got colder. She pushed her head out through the bottom of the doggie door just as Skeeter disappeared down the concrete stairs. Just as Thena started to yell for Skeeter to get back into the house, the flap banged back down, forcing Thena's head back into the kitchen. "This just isn't going my way!" Thena's yell echoed throughout the room.

Deciding to take another approach to the matter, Thena hunkered down, jumped, and threw her entire body weight into the flap. The doggie door pushed back against her, but her momentum carried her through the opening into the harsh mid-morning sunlight. She landed on all four legs, hitting the hard concrete with a thud. Her eyes quickly adjusted to the light, and she scanned the areal looking for her target as the feeling came back to her legs from the hard landing. Thena was standing on a short set of concrete steps from the house to the backyard. The grass was a deep green with yellow and white wild flowers growing sporadically throughout the yard. A flower bed ran through the middle of the widest part of the yard, with tall, beautiful flowers in various shades of red, yellow, and deep purple. A tall white fence surrounded the lush grass, and tall trees at the far end of the yard darkened the horizon as they spread out their shade in both directions. A short distance from the bottom step, Thena spotted her target rolling around in the grass. To Thena's surprise, it brought a smile to her face to see the rat rolling around in the yard. It reminded her of Ebony.

Ebony had been the family dog when Thena joined them four years ago. She had been a loyal companion to all the members of the family, especially the mother, wagging her tail excitedly with her claws clicking on the hardwood floors when any member of the family came home.

Ebony had been a "grass roller." That's what the family called it when she would roll around in the grass on a bright summer day. Some days Max would sit on the back step with Thena for hours watching the dog roll around in the grass until she finally fell asleep. Thena especially missed those days where Max would let her crawl around all day, and she would spend most of her time cuddled under the dog's long fur like it was a dark, warm cave.

After about three years, the family took Ebony somewhere and didn't return with her. Thena could see how upset the family had been, tears streaming down their cheeks. She had learned to recognize the red in a human's eyes that represented pain. Even the Dad, who always seemed so reserved to Thena, had tears in his eyes. She heard the family talk about cancer or something like that, but all she could make out of it was that the fluffy black dog was going to die so they made her go to sleep and she would never wake up again. Thena couldn't imagine falling asleep and never waking up. It gave her chills just thinking about it.

Watching Skeeter roll around in the grass brought back those old feelings again. Those had been the good days. After Ebony was put to sleep, Max seemed to grow up more quickly, having less and less time for Thena. She smiled again at the rat before a motion overhead caught her eye. At first it disappeared behind the bright sun, but then she could see a shadow circle back over to the spot where Skeeter was rolling around in the grass. She had been born and raised in a cage so her survival instincts were not what they were supposed to be, but something in Thena triggered an alarm as the shadow got closer and closer to Skeeter.

Thena tried to yell but her mouth felt dry and wouldn't form the words she wanted. Panic rose up inside her as the shadow took on the form of a large brown bird. It was the biggest bird that she had ever seen. A sudden realization hit her when she remembered seeing a picture of this bird in a book Max left lying around. It was a hawk, and a hawk's main source of food was small rodents!

"Skeeter, watch out!" Thena finally managed to shout.

Skeeter turned and smiled at Thena, but the massive bird swooped down and grabbed the small rat in its large, razor sharp talons before she could say another word. Large brown wings beat at the air, kicking up grass and small white petals from nearby wildflowers. Thena could feel the wind on her face as the massive bird carried its prey higher into the air. All she could do was watch in horror as the massive, scary bird carried her friend away.

Thena yelled Skeeter's name over and over again even though she knew it was useless, as the bird and its prey flew further and further away. Even if her friend could hear her, Thena doubted that there was anything that could have been done. Thena's whole body went numb, and her limbs went limp. Her heart beat so fast she thought it would explode out of her chest, and she felt like everything she ate that morning was going to come back up. Thena knew it had been a bad idea to leave the tank but she never expected something like this! With every minute that passed, the bird was further away, and any hope Thena had of seeing the rat again drifted away just as swiftly.

Just when Thena was about to give up completely and head back to the safety of the house, she saw another bird swoop down on the brown hawk. It was bigger than the brown hawk, and black as night with white-tipped wings and white feathers around its head. The two birds of prey collided in an impressive display of aerial combat, a spray of feathers, locked talons, and violence. Thena couldn't make out much from a distance, but just as the birds collided she could see the outline of a small object dropping quickly through the air and into the trees below. She knew it had been Skeeter. That lucky little rat always found a way out of things! Even if Skeeter had nothing to do with the escape, it just figured that she would find a way out.

Thena knew she had to go look for Skeeter. She hated the thought of the poor little rat all alone, and, judging from the distance she had fallen, Skeeter was most likely hurt also. Thena eyed the trees beyond the yard. The thick brown trunks reached the sky, with branches so heavy with leaves she couldn't distinguish one tree from the other. The trees trailed off in every direction, even further than Thena could see. This wasn't going to be easy at all! But Thena knew there was no way she could go back inside without her friend. Amyah would be heartbroken if the rat never came back, and Thena wanted to prevent another family heartbreak if she could. This family deserved better.

Thena watched for a few minutes until the two large birds disappeared further into the sky, then she jumped down the stairs and made her way across the yard. Skeeter wanted some adventure, and now she had it. Skeeter actually opened up a whole heap of adventure, which was sure to give them both a whole lifetime of bad dreams and scars. Once again, Thena reminded herself to give the pesky little rat a firm talking to when she found her, as Skeeter was definitely not getting off easy this time, no matter how cute and innocent she tried to look. Thena eyeballed the spot above the trees where she thought the rat fell, then set her course for that point. She had to get Skeeter home, no matter what!

Chapter Six

A New Friend

It was hard for Skeeter to open her eyes at first since they felt heavier than usual, and her head hurt so bad it felt like it was split open. Eventually, the blackness of her vision receded and gave way to a foggy grey haze that allowed Skeeter to see a few blurry outlines and faint colors. Her ability to hear sounds reappeared almost all at once, making her head hurt even worse. Sharp, crisp bird whistles, the croaking of tree frogs, and the constant yapping of dogs off in the distance crashed against her eardrums, a chaos of sound. She focused as hard as she could on just the highest notes of the birds so she could master the chaos, get her mind oriented. It eventually paid off, as all of the jumbled noises ceased their pounding against her skull and she began to think more clearly. Even her foggy vision cleared up, which allowed Skeeter a first look at her surroundings. She was surrounded by tall, dark trees that tangled together in a dense, overlapping canopy that allowed only the occasional ray of light through. The ground underneath her was hard and dry with only a rare piece of greenery poking through.

Skeeter tried to recall how she ended up here, but the last thing she could remember was the bird grabbing her. Fear seized her again when she merely thought about the large bird with its razor-like talons digging into her sides. She scanned the sky, but all she could see was tree branches blocking the light. Not seeing the sky made her feel safer for a moment. She figured there was no way a bird that big could fly under all these trees so she tried to relax and let her body recuperate from the day's events.

How could this have happened? All Skeeter wanted was to experience something new and maybe have a little excitement. This was way more than she wanted, especially getting carried away by some monster bird and dropped here.

The Case of the Curious Rat

Where am I, Skeeter wondered. Obviously, she was in the woods, but just how far from home was she? Why did every muscle and bone from her nose to her tail hurt so badly? The feeling was gradually returning to her trunk and extremities, but pain shot through her muscles whenever she tried to stretch her legs. She must have taken a beating because even the tip of her tail was in pain!

"Feeling better?" An unknown voice squeaked its inquiry from somewhere nearby. Skeeter quickly tucked herself into a hollow space in a nearby tree and tried to make herself as small and invisible as possible.

"Don't worry. I'm not going to hurt you. I just thought I'd see if you were OK." Skeeter scanned the area, but couldn't find the source of the voice. She knew she had to be careful out here, or she would never make it home.

"Sooo, are you?" The squeaky voice asked again.

"Am I what?" Skeeter was wary of the little nosy voice.

"Are you ok? I saw you fall out of the trees. By the way, that was one heck of a fall! I thought you might have been dead at first, but then you started moving around a bit."

"You saw me fall?"

"Oh yeah, you fell out of that tree that you're hiding under. Did you jump or were you pushed out?"

"Well, I don't remember how I got down here." Skeeter was puzzled. "The last thing I remember was a huge bird grabbing me, and…wait a minute, where are you? Can you come out so I can see you? It's kind of weird talking to nothing."

A few seconds passed with no answer, but then a small brown animal with a black stripe running down its back emerged from the bush right in front of Skeeter without moving a single branch. Skeeter admired the amount of talent it took to sneak around that quietly.

"There you are," Skeeter said, with a hint of admiration for the creature's stealthy moves.

"Here I am, and the name's Jay by the way." The small, brown chipmunk introduced himself with a bow.

"I'm Skeeter." She wanted to make a grand

move with her introduction, but the pain would not allow it.

"Skeeter? That's a funny name. So, how did you end up way out here falling out of trees?"

"Well, like I said, I don't remember how I got out here. The last thing I remember was being grabbed by a large bird and then I woke up here."

"Well, it sounds like you may have gotten a little lucky then." Jay scratched behind his tiny ears quickly before standing on his hind legs and scanning the area for any potential threat. "Yup, lucky indeed. So, I'm guessing you're not from around here. Where are you from?"

"Guess I don't really know where I'm from. I live with a human family in a house."

"Ahhh, you live in one of the houses." Jay was impressed. "Well, that must be interesting. I don't get too close to the houses personally, but I've known others that have done it. Boy, do they have stories to tell!"

"Well, I like my home and I need to get back there fast, so I'd appreciate it if you could just point me in the right direction." Skeeter started to feel a bit anxious about being away.

"Oh, my! Well, the houses are that way," Jay pointed his tail in a direction over Skeeter's shoulder, "but you should wait until morning to head there. It's a long way off and it'll be dark soon. Trust me when I say you don't want to be stuck out here after dark."

Skeeter firmly agreed with the chipmunk. As much as her new surroundings scared her now, she hated to think what it would be like after dark. She wished she had listened to that grumpy lizard and not gone down the stairs. Skeeter hated to admit it, but Thena had been right. Nothing good had come out of venturing down the stairs, and Skeeter was certain that Thena would be all to glad to remind her when or if she got back home. Skeeter sighed heavily.

Jay noticed Skeeter's sigh, and wanted to give her some comfort. "Well, if you'd like to, you can stay with me and my family for tonight then head out in the morning. I could even take you some of the way back towards your house, but we don't get too close to the houses so you'd be on your own once we got near there."

It scared Skeeter to think that she had to spend the night out here in the woods, but she figured being safely inside with Jay and his family would be better than in the woods on her own. This was especially true since Skeeter was not moving very well at the moment. A good night's sleep would probably work wonders on her aching muscles.

"Ok, as long as it'll be fine with your family." Skeeter didn't want to impose on a den full of creatures she hardly knew.

"Oh, it'll be fine. My parents love company! Plus, you don't look like you eat a whole lot. Or do you? Eat a whole lot, I mean."

"Umm, I don't think so, but I don't have a whole lot to judge my eating against. Maybe I do and I just don't know it. Thena always said…" Skeeter stopped suddenly, mid-sentence. A long silence stretched on as she realized she was about to start rambling. Jay had his head cocked to one side just like Thena always did when listening to Skeeter ramble on. It made her miss the grumpy lizard even more. "No, I don't eat a whole lot, but I would like to stay the night with you and your family," she finally said.

"Good, so let's get going then." Jay scratched himself behind his ear one more time, and darted under the bush where he had appeared earlier. Skeeter hated that they set off away from the direction leading to the houses, according to Jay's earlier comment, but she figured the quick talking chipmunk knew what he was doing.

"Not too fast, I'm still a little sore," she managed to say before Jay disappeared completely under the bush.

She followed as quickly as she could, her legs cramping from the exercise that her body clearly wasn't ready for. Each time Skeeter took a step her legs felt like there were going to give out. She had to mentally will her legs to keep moving, push herself to keep going. Jay made it easy for her to keep up. Just when she thought she would get left behind she would emerge from under a bush or around a tree trunk and find Jay waiting patiently for her to catch up. He was quick and agile while moving along the floor of the woods, barely making a sound as they raced toward their destination. Skeeter supposed if she had been healthy she would have had no problem keeping up with the chipmunk, but doubted she could make less noise moving through the dense underbrush.

"We're here!" Jay made his pronouncement after he stopped at the base of a very, very large tree. Skeeter had a nice view from the window in Amyah's room but had never seen a tree as big as this one before. The base of the trunk was so big around that she couldn't see around either side of it. It towered above the surrounding trees like a giant. "Now, we go up."

"Up?" Skeeter was slightly confused. "You really live up there, up this huge tree?"

"Sure do! Best view in the woods!" Jay put his paws on the tree and began to climb. "Can you make it?" Jay started his scamper up the tree with ease.

"Of course, I can." Skeeter replied, trying to suppress the hint of anger in her voice from Jay's question.

Jay kept the climbing pace nice and easy so Skeeter wouldn't fall behind. She found that by the time they stopped climbing at a large branch, her legs were no longer cramping and her head barely hurt. She had even started to keep up with Jay, climbing side by side. Skeeter glanced around her, taking in the beauty of the forest, and found that the large branch they were on extended out from high above the tops of all the other surrounding trees. It felt like forever since Skeeter last saw the sun, and it felt good to have it shining on her face again, melting her headache away and warming her fur. Birds and brightly colored butterflies hovered over the tree tops. This had to be one of the most beautiful sights Skeeter had ever seen.

"You're right, Jay. It is the best view in the forest." Skeeter was impressed.

"Told you so," Jay said with a smile.

Skeeter and Jay heard a commotion above them in the tree and they both looked up. Two squirrels, one big with a wide fluffy tail, the other as thin as a pencil with a tail that looked like it had been cut short, were a few branches higher up arguing over a really large nut in the thin one's hands.

"Don't be silly! Of course, it's not real! How many times I gotta tell you that?!" The bigger squirrel looked exasperated, and they could hear it in his deep voice.

"Yeah, uh-huh, it is real! Don't be jealous because I found it and you didn't!" The thinner squirrel hugged the giant acorn close. He sounded like a little kid after sucking in the air from a helium balloon.

"Why do you have to embarrass me like this all the time? IT'S FAKE!!" The bigger squirrel's voice boomed through the air, shaking a flurry of leaves free from their branches. Skeeter could tell they had been going at it for a while from the sound of his voice. "Just take a bite, then. Go on, you'll see."

"No way, no how! I'm saving this little beauty for the winter! And when you're nice and hungry don't think I'll be giving you a bite." The thinner squirrel looked so smug.

Booming voice smacked his head at the smaller squirrels comment, but Jay interrupted before he could continue. "Oh, hey guys. This is Skeeter. She's new to the log. Skeeter, that's Ham," Jay pointed to the bigger of the two "and that's Bean," he gestured to the thinner squirrel. "They're brothers."

Skeeter had a good idea which one was Ham and which was Bean just by the size difference between the two.

"Oh, hey, Jay," the squirrels said, almost simultaneously. "Hey, Skeeter, and welcome to the log."

"Hello," Skeeter replied. "Nice to meet you."

"You see," Ham turned back to his brother, "now Jay and his new friend know how stupid you can be."

"Ohhh, really?! That's it now, you've gone too far! Nobody calls me stupid, not even you!" Bean was enraged.

"Oh, yeah?! What you gonna do about it Pee Wee?" Ham said.

Bean stood up on his back legs, stretched to his full height, and quickly circled his brother, paws jabbing out threateningly. He only came up to the middle of Ham's chest despite standing up on his two hind legs. Skeeter wanted to laugh at the sight but didn't want to offend the smaller squirrel or make him any angrier.

"Oh, boy! I'm scared now!" Ham just sat there shaking his head.

"I know you are!" Bean was livid. "Don't pretend you're not just because someone is watching!"

Jay turned to Skeeter and rolled his eyes. "We

should get going. They could be at it for a while."

Skeeter was nervous. "Shouldn't we put a stop to this? Ham could really hurt him."

"Oh, Ham would never hurt Bean. This is just what they do. Soon, Bean will get tired of circling Ham, then Ham will apologize for whatever it is that made Bean mad, and then a couple hours later they'll start up again over something else. It's pretty funny sometimes."

Skeeter figured she would take Jay's word for it since he knew the brothers, but it still seemed like an odd relationship to her.

"What's the log?" Skeeter wondered what "the log" meant.

"Oh, that's what we call the tree," Jay explained. "Kind of a funny name, huh, for such a big tree."

"Sure is," Skeeter agreed.

"Ok, guys see you later," Jay yelled to the brothers. Neither one paid any attention since they were back to arguing. Bean had even started to bob and weave as he circled the bigger squirrel.

Skeeter followed her new friend into a hole that

led deep into the tree. Jay had no problem crawling through. Skeeter, being a little bigger around than the chipmunk, didn't have it as easy. At one point, she had to suck herself in and become as small as possible to fit through, even though her belly still slid along the tunnel floor and her head occasionally bumped the roof. She could see why they had made their home here. The opening was hidden enough for most to move right past it without ever noticing it, while small enough to keep most predators out.

After a short time, the tunnel opened into a large cavern with a warm, inviting feeling to it. Rays of sunlight shone through tiny holes, giving the room plenty of light. At the far end was a large pile of nuts and berries, most of them kinds that Skeeter had never seen before, though they smelled like they would be quite edible and delicious. Two smaller chipmunks were chasing each other in and out of the large cavern through a series of side tunnels, their squeaky voices echoing around the chamber. Jay's mom sat in the middle of the cavern, giving a slightly chunkier young chipmunk with bulging cheeks a tongue bath.

"Come on, mom, I already had a bath today!"

The chubby little sibling pled with his mom and tried to escape from her licks. "Isn't it time to eat yet?" He wiggled and squirmed in her arms.

"Hush now, you know you haven't had a bath today! Besides, I'm almost done." Jay's mom scolded the chubby squirrel.

"Aww, mom, come on..."

"Mom, I'm home," Jay interrupted.

"Good," his mom answered between licks, "and I see that you brought a stray home with you."

"Yeah, I found her in the woods," Jay explained. "She managed to escape from a hawk after it grabbed her."

"Really?! That sounds amazing!" Jay's sibling seized the opportunity to escape the bath to run down the nearest tunnel, joining its kin in the chase. Skeeter wanted to laugh while watching the chubby little guy waddle after his sibling.

"Does your friend have a name?" Jay's mom just grinned at the waddling chubby youngster.

Jay introduced Skeeter to his mom, who everyone just called Momma K. The older chipmunk greeted her with a warm smile and welcomed her to their home. She even insisted that Skeeter stay the night, no questions asked. She had never met a chipmunk before Jay and his family, but Momma K was probably the prettiest she thought she would ever meet. She had long fluffy brown fur with just a hint of grey that looked like she spent the better part of the day taking care of it, with a thick black strip that went from her head to her tail. She also had big black eyes that made Skeeter feel at home. It was no wonder she felt so at ease around Jay, as she realized he had the same warm, caring eyes as Momma K.

After she rounded the three younger siblings up, they all sat in a circle eating colorful berries and hard-shelled nuts that the family gathered every morning. Skeeter liked the flavor of the fresh berries, especially the round red ones and the purple ones with all the little bumps all over. Even though the nuts were a little harder for her to get open, they had a nice, meatier taste than the ones she got at home. Momma K introduced her to Jay's sister May and her twin brothers, Huey and Pudge, the youngest whose cheeks were already puffed out with food. "Nice to meet you," they all said, as crumbs of food kept falling out of Pudge's mouth.

They asked Skeeter to tell them all about what it was like living in a house, so she told them about her big multi-leveled cage, and all the different foods and snacks she ate. She even told them all about how Thena was her best friend, which made them all laugh because they had never met a rat with a lizard for a best friend. She even told them about the family and how wonderful her girl Amyah was, but when Skeeter started to tell them about all the different food the little girl would share with her Pudge could no long contain his excitement. He asked question after question, never giving Skeeter time to answer him.

"Wait, how big is pepperoni pizza? Do ramen noodles really taste like chicken? Wait, what's chicken? Chocolate sounds wonderful! Tell me again about cheesy puffs!" Tiny crumbs and drops of his fruit juice fell from Pudge's mouth with every word.

But it wasn't until Skeeter started talking about being snatched by the bird that the other two chipmunks started to pay attention. They listened wide-eyed as she told them about the huge claws that held her so tight she passed out, and its mighty wings beating the air like giant fans. They asked her all kinds of questions about how she got away, what kind of bird it was and how she had survived the fall, though she didn't have any answers for them. They protested in anger when Momma K finally told them it was time for bed and accused Skeeter of withholding information from them because they were little.

"But mom, I don't want to go to bed! We need to go find some pizza!" Pudge protested to Momma K. "Maybe we could go with Skeeter when she leaves. Don't cheesy puffs sound wonderful?"

It made Skeeter laugh when she thought about Amyah coming home from school and finding a family of chipmunks in the cage. It took Momma K a while, but finally she got the three younger chipmunks settled down for the night. She said good night to Jay and Skeeter and disappeared down another tunnel.

"Well, I think I'm going to go to sleep too," Skeeter said after a few brief seconds of silence.

"Yeah, ok. See you in the morning, Skeeter."

Jay sounded pretty tired, and didn't go too far away. He snuggled up near the tunnel to the outside and fell right asleep. Skeeter lay awake for some time, thinking about what it was like to sit and talk as a family. She loved how they ate together, joked around, and even how the younger kids chased each other around. She loved Amyah so much, but seeing the chipmunk family made her miss the rat tanks she lived in early on. It made her miss being with family, how close they were, and the love they shared.

Chapter Seven.

A Tunnel to Nowhere

Thena lowered herself as close to the black dirt of the flower garden as she could. She was in her element now. Tall, colorful flowers bloomed around her and the soft dirt was cool on her exposed belly. Thena was surrounded by the sounds of the outdoors. Somewhere in the distance, dogs barked at anyone that got too close, birds chirped from their perches high in the trees, and buzzing insects flew through the air to their destinations. She was one with her prey now as she watched the small beetle scurrying closer to her. Just a little closer, she thought, just a little closer…

She struck the black bug before it even knew

she was there, savoring its juicy flavor as it slid down her throat into her stomach. Thena always knew she was a great hunter and proved it as she hunted the bugs of the outdoors. They tried to be sneaky, and actually were sneakier than the bugs Max fed to her, but they all met the same fate in the end. No matter where they hid or how quiet they tried to be they always ended up as dinner. Dinner for the mighty hunter.

Thena stalked a couple more of the small black bugs until her belly was full, but she took care not to get too full in case she had to make a quick escape. She decided to lay out on a flat rock bathed in sunlight and sun herself after her meal.

This is the life, she thought to herself. Between hunting, basking under real sunlight, and enjoying the breeze and creature sounds, Thena was definitely starting to see the appeal of living outside.

After a short period of basking under the warm sun, Thena felt her body temperature return to normal. She slid off the rock to continue her Skeeter rescue mission. She poked her head in between the stems of two tall flowers with wide yellow petals to scan the last half of the yard. It was just as open as the first half, with green grass cut short, and a total lack of any trees or shrubs that could be used for cover. Thena looked up at the sun which was now past the mid-day point. She knew there were only a couple more hours left of sunlight and it would take at least that amount of time to cross the yard at the speed she needed to go.

Thena took her time getting to the flower garden that grew in the middle of the family's yard, being extra careful the whole way in case any predators were hanging around, stealthily sliding through the short grass while scanning her surroundings the whole way. She thought she could find Skeeter and return home before dark but now realized that it wasn't going to happen. She had taken too long to get across the first half of the yard, and then got caught up in hunting for something to eat. It would likely be well into the night before she found her friend.

Thena dug her claws into the black soil in aggravation. She had been too careful and it had cost her valuable time and daylight. I need a new plan, she thought.

Maybe she could just make a run for it, just run as fast as she could, not stopping for anything until she got to the woods. Thena heard a loud screech overhead and thought she saw a shadow pass over the grass in front of her. She looked up but couldn't see anything through the flowers. The next screech seemed so close it made the air around Thena vibrate. The hawk had come back to look for its lunch and Thena wasn't about to make herself the main course. She would just have to wait until the bird of prey moved on before making a run for it, costing her even more time.

"You best wait for that bigg'un to leave before you go out there." Thena jumped at the sound of a new voice and quickly turned to confront the newcomer. By reflex, her beard bulged out like a balloon and she opened her mouth threateningly.

"Whoa! Hold on there a sec, missy. I'm not gonna hurt you. I just saw you lookin' like you were thinking about goin' out there. Didn't mean to scare you."

Thena had always enjoyed looking through the animal books Max had, learning all about the different animals around the world. He even had a book on bearded dragons where she learned a lot about herself, like how she was originally from a place called Australia. But Thena had never seen an animal like this! It stood a little shorter than a house cat but had grayish armor all over its body.

"What are you?" Her mouth was dry, making it hard to say much else.

"Me? Well, heck! Missy, I'm an armadillo." His voice sounded like the cowboys from those TV shows.

"Armadillo?"

"Sure thing, little lady! Name's Hank the Tank, but people just call me Tank. It's a pleasure to meet you."

"I'm Thena," she relaxed her beard since she could see now that he wasn't a threat. "Nice to meet you, too."

A small smile spread underneath his long nose. "Well, like I said, I would wait until the Hawk leaves before going out there, but that's just my opinion."

"Thanks, but I don't have time to waste."

"Well, missy, I don't know what you got goin' on, but it can't be so important that you have to go on out there and get yourself killed over it." Tank lowered his body down to the ground so the armor on his body covered his legs. She noticed that he had a laid back way about him, like he was never in a hurry to be anywhere.

"Thanks, but I'll manage," Thena said, just as another screech vibrated through the air as if to call her a liar.

"I'm sure you can." Tank's whole body leaned to one side to emphasize his more laid back attitude. "What's your story, missy? What's so important that you'll risk being lunch to get to there?"

Thena didn't really have the time to explain, but figured a few more minutes wouldn't hurt since the Hawk was still hovering around. Tank listened intently as Thena told him about Skeeter going outside, and how Thena had foolishly gone after the rat. She told him how the Hawk grabbed Skeeter, and then dropped her out in the woods when another bird swooped in and attacked the Hawk. She explained how important it was to find Skeeter, not only to Thena but to the little girl Skeeter belonged to so it needed to get done quickly. When Thena was finished, she thought Tank had fallen asleep because his eyes looked closed. When she went to poke him, he jumped up and said "Ok, I think I have something for you."

"What do you mean you have something for me?" Thena was uncertain.

"Follow me," was all Tank said, and then waddled off.

She easily followed Tank since he walked like he was never in a hurry, and after a short distance he stopped next to a hole in the ground. The hole was dark and damp and dropped down a short distance before trailing off in one direction. Small roots stuck out of the sides of the tunnel in random places.

"Here you go, missy." Tank had a satisfied look on his face.

"What is it?" Thena was uncertain.

"The rabbits use it. It's a tunnel that goes from here into the woods somewhere, all underground. It's safer than running across open ground, I think."

Thena sat looking down the hole, stunned. If she could take this tunnel all the way into the woods, it would save her so much time! With luck, she could find Skeeter today, and they could start

The Case of the Curious Rat

making their way home!

"Oh, Tank! Thank you so much! This is perfect!" Thena started to head down the hole before Tank stopped her by nudging his long head in her way.

"Need to warn you missy. It may be faster, but you still need to be careful. I hear that sometimes a snake will decide to make himself comfy down there and that always ends badly for whoever comes across it." Tank had a look of concern on his face. "I'd go with you, but it's a little too small for me. Besides, I get a little goofy in tight spaces."

"I'll be ok," she said. "Again, thank you so much, Tank. This is a huge help." Thena smiled at the armadillo. "I'll remember this always."

"No problem, little missy! You just be careful, and I hope you find that friend of yours."

She gave Tank one last smile and jumped down the hole. It was a short distance to the bottom and the loose dirt cushioned her landing. Bits of dirt fell on her head, so Thena looked up and saw Tank peering down into the hole until his head finally disappeared. A tight beam of sunlight peeked through the flowers in the garden overhead and blinded Thena for a second before disappearing behind some clouds. Yellow spots flashed in front of her eyes, so she closed her eyes until they adjusted to the normal light in the tunnel. She could see only a short distance down the tunnel before the weak light that shone down the tunnel gradually gave way to complete darkness.

"This should he interesting," Thena said and her voice echoed down the hall.

She set off down the tunnel at a nice jog, dodging the occasional root creeping across the tunnel's floor or hanging low from overhead. Even with her night vision, she still managed to bump her head or trip over an occasional root. It wasn't long before she started to feel the exhaustion from running, her lungs on fire and her legs cramping. She dropped her speed to a quick walk, but soon even that became tiring. She was definitely out of shape from years of basking in her tank and decided that she was going to start exercising more often, even if it was only a couple of laps around the terrarium. The burning finally disappeared from her lungs and her legs no longer cramped, but the slower pace was going to cost her a lot of valuable time. Time she didn't think she could spare.

Smaller tunnels ran off into the darkness sporadically on either side of the main tunnel, some no bigger than Skeeter, others wide enough to fit an entire family of rats walking side by side. She hated to think where some of the passageways would take her, or if she could even find her way back if she wandered down one, so Thena decided that it would be best to stick to the main tunnel. She would be no good to anyone if she got herself lost down in a maze of underground tunnels for days.

After what felt like forever, surrounded in darkness with nothing but her own thoughts for companionship, she spotted a faint light off in the distance. It was hard to tell how far away it was, but the light gave her renewed vigor and she moved a little quicker than before. Gradually, the spot of light got bigger and bigger until she could finally see a hole in the roof and a dim circle of light on the tunnel floor. Her heart raced at the prospect of being under the sun again after all the time spent in blackness.

Small bits of dirt fell from the opening in the ceiling, and as the crumbs tumbled down the walls, they sent larger bits of loose dirt tumbling down too. A long, dark shadow blocked out some of the light also, freezing Thena in her tracks. Any sort of creature could have been up there, but for some reason Thena had a sick feeling it wasn't going to be a friendly creature. Thena slowly backed into the shadows and ducked behind a large root. More dirt bounced down the tunnel's walls followed by a slender black shadow. Yellow eyes glistened in the darkness, darting left and right while searching for any intruders. The black snake lowered itself slowly to the floor of the tunnel, its broad, flat head darkening the tunnel as more and more of its body came slithering through the opening.

Thena's legs shook with fear. She had never imagined a snake so long! She saw pictures in Max's reptile books of snakes from all over the world, but the pictures never made them seem very big. The snake's fat, round body finally ended with a slim tail that darted through the darkness next to the head for a bit before the snake withdrew it and curled his tail up under the black mass of his reptilian body. Its yellow eyes scanned the darkness, and its tongue flicked out rapidly, tasting the moist air.

Thena quietly backed deeper into the tunnel to get as much room as she could between her and the black predator. Every step backward was slow and deliberate so as not to disturb any lose dirt or a stray root. To her left, slightly hidden beneath a clump of tangled roots, Thena could see the outline of a small opening underneath. She carefully tried to nudge the roots aside with her head, but a large clump of dirt wiggled loose and crashed to the tunnel floor, sending smaller clumps and chunks scattering in every direction. Thena froze in fear as the snake's black head turned in her direction, yellow eyes piercing the blackness. Those yellow eyes seemed to look right through her.

Less worried about noise and more worried about getting somewhere safe, Thena quickly backed into the smaller tunnel. It was a tight fit but she managed to squeeze in and hunker down in it as far as she could. Her spikes dug into her sides and her legs were trapped underneath her. A black form slithered slowly past the tunnel, never noticing her hiding place. Thena wondered if she should make a run for it while the monster was off in the other direction, but quickly decided against it when a loud hiss vibrated through the tunnel.

"I knowsss you're in here, little bug." The hissing voice echoed down the tunnel. "I can ssssmell your fear."

Thena's body shook and her mouth felt dry hearing the slick predator's voice as it slithered closer. Could it really smell her fear? If so, how could she possibly hide from an animal with such abilities? She closed her eyes and tried to calm down by taking short deep breaths but the tunnel was too tight. She wiggled her way toward the opening to give herself a bit of breathing room, and gradually felt the pressure letting up.

"I sssee you." Thena opened her eyes and saw two evil yellow eyes staring back at her, with a forked tongue flicking toward her direction. "I think I've ssssmelled every animal in these woods but you ssssmell different, sssssomething I've never ssssmelled before. Why don't you come on out of there little bug sssso I can have a look at you."

"I'm fine right here, thank you." Thena's mouth felt like it was filled with cotton, and her voice cracked with strain.

"Oh, come on now, little bug, come on out here

ssso I can take a look at you. I promissse I won't hurt you." Thena could see the forked tongue flicking toward her down the tunnel. Those yellow eyes never stopped staring, sizing Thena up. "Come on now, little bug, don't be rude. I keep my word."

Thena doubted very much that she would feel safe if she came out of the tunnel despite what the yellow eyed snake said, and she had no intention of finding out.

"It seems I'm a little stuck right now, so perhaps we could have our little face to face some other time. I could take a rain check if you'd like. Two weeks from today would be good for me," Thena lied.

"Awww, don't you trussst me little bug? I'm more than a little curious about what sssort of animal you are. You sssmell like a reptile, but not like one I've ever met."

"So you'll just let me go on my way when you find out what kind of reptile I am? For some reason I seriously doubt it will be that easy." Thena was wary of the snake's fake-friendly conversation.

"Are you calling me a liar, little bug?" The

snakes yellow eyes seemed to glow at the end of the tunnel in anger.

"I'm a bearded dragon, not a bug, so would you please stop calling me one." Thena was a bit incensed herself.

"Ah, you're a bearded dragon? Well, well, I can't sssay that I've ever heard of one before, but then I haven't been very far from thisss area either." The black head squeezed into the opening of the tunnel. "Now come on out of there! I am a sssnake of my word."

"As I said before I seem to be stuck but..." Thena began.

"That isss the sssecond time you have called me a liar to my face, little bug! There won't be a third if you know whatsss good for you." Thena could feel the anger dripping off the snake's forked tongue and its black scales seemed to ripple in response. "If you insist on calling me a liar, I think we will have a problem. Ssso what'sss it gonna be, bearded dragon?"

Thena didn't want to make the snake any angrier by telling him she thought he was lying about being a liar, but at this point it almost seemed unavoidable.

"It's not that I think you're a liar. It's just that I'm new to the outside and really have trust issues when I meet new people, so it's, err, nothing personal." The black predator seemed to settle down a bit as Thena spoke.

"Hmmm, ssso you're a house reptile then? I've met a few in my day, all sssnakesss of courssse. They don't tend to lassst very long out here. Isss that what happened to you, little bearded dragon? Did your owner ssset you out in the cold, cruel world with nothing but your lazy indoor hunting skills to sssurvive on?" A small smile spread slowly underneath the yellow eyes. "Isss that what you are? Sssome lazy houssse pet doomed to die from ssstarvation?"

Thena could feel her cheeks heat up and was thankful for the darkness since she was sure they were also red. What would this slimy bottom feeder know about living in a house? Ok, so maybe she didn't have to rely on catching food for herself, but in the short time she had been outside she has already proven herself as both a hunter and a survivor.

"Actually, I came outside on my own looking for a friend, and I seem to be doing just fine on my own."

"Oh, you are indeed, ssstuck in there like sssome poor pathetic rat." High pitched laughter escaped through the snake's black lips and echoed through Thena's small tunnel. The snake coiled up into itself, laughing and sputtering. "Woohoo! I haven't laughed that hard in a long time!" He said. "Not doing ssso bad? Well, I guess I ssshould give you sssome credit. At least you haven't ssstarved to death yet!"

Thena decided that arguing with the snake would be useless and only make her even angrier. "Ok, you know what I am now, so there is no need for us to continue this conversation, if you don't mind?" Thena tried to sound polite. "So if we could both just go on our own way that would be fine by me."

"I'm sssure it would be fine, but you amussse me too much little beardy! Plus, I have all the time in the world to wait for you to come out of your little hole." Once again, black lips peeled back into a vicious smile this time, exposing large white fangs that seemed to glow in the pitch black tunnel.

"Well, I guess this is going to be a long night." Thena said this just softly enough that her captor turned its head questioningly toward her. This is all Skeeter's fault. Thena thought this again, but this time she wasn't quite sure if she meant it.

Chapter Eight

Run Away, Home

Skeeter watched the sun peek over the horizon in awe. Rays of sunlight bathed the treetops and glistened off of the tiled roofs of homes in the distance, as she wondered if one of the homes was hers. A humming bird flittered past her face, its wings beating so fast that it appeared the bird was actually wingless. It hovered close to a long tree limb for a second before disappearing further down the tree. Light, fluffy clouds floated along in the bright blue sky. It made her wish the view from Amyah's room was this spectacular. It was early in the day, and the "log" was just coming to life.

Jay's siblings were a couple of branches up, chasing each other around the trunk of the tree, hollering back and forth about who was and was not out. A couple of other families were coming out of the trunk at lower levels of the tree for their morning routines.

"It's amazing, isn't it?" Skeeter was surprised when she turned to see Ham, the larger of the two Squirrel brothers, standing behind her admiring the same sunrise. It still amazed her how such a deep voice came from such a small body.

"It sure is," she replied.

"So, Jay tells me you're going to try and get back home today. You have any idea how to get there?"

"Well, not really….I sort of thought we would start from the place Jay found me and work from there. I can't imagine it being too hard to find." In reality, Skeeter had no idea at all how to get home but didn't want to openly admit it.

"Yeah, well, the houses aren't that hard to find, which is true, but you could be looking for a while unless you know what color the house is and can recognize it from the outside."

It irritated Skeeter that Ham was right. She had gone outside with such reckless abandon she hadn't even bothered noticing what color the house was.

"Sorry, I didn't mean to sound so negative." Ham must have sensed her irritation.

"It's ok," Skeeter's whiskers twitched nervously, "but I have to at least try to get home."

"Skeeter, I know we just met but you are welcome to stay here. The log offers protection from the dangers of the woods, and we are all one big family. We could be your family now."

The idea of having a family again sounded wonderful. The night with Jay's family had been a wonderful experience that she would always remember, but Skeeter needed to get home to Amyah because she knew the little girl would be lost without her. She could feel her eyes getting wet just remembering her favorite little girl with the long, golden curls.

"That sounds great, but I need to get home. My little girl will be heartbroken if I don't show up. She's almost certainly noticed that I'm missing by now, and is probably making herself sick with worry about where I've gone. I have to get back to her."

"Well, you always have a home here," Ham said with a smile.

"Trying to talk her into staying?" Jay poked his head out of a hole in the tree.

"Yeah, I'm trying, but she seems set in her ways," Ham smiled again.

"Well, can't say that I'm surprised, and that's what I was just coming out here to talk to her about," Jay said.

"I'm sorry, but I need to get back. My little girl needs me, and Thena probably thinks I'm dead and it wouldn't be fair to not let her know I'm alright."

"Like I said," Jay continued, "I'm not surprised. I kind of knew you would say something like that."

"Wait, who is Thena?" Ham interrupted.

"Long story, Ham. I'll tell you later." Jay looked at Skeeter. "Well, we should get going if we're going to get you back to the houses by dark. Trust me; we don't want to be out in the woods when the sun goes down."

"Getting to the houses before dark isn't really

gonna be the problem. How do you think you will possibly make it back here to the log before dark, Jay?" Ham's booming voice echoed his concern.

"Don't worry about me," Jay said. "I have a hidey hole close to the houses that I can stay in for the night. No problem." Jay's whiskers twitched as he winked at Skeeter.

"Well, if you think you're ok, I'll let you guys get to it. Just remember Skeeter, you are always welcome here." Ham gave Skeeter one last long look and a smile.

"Thanks, Ham, I will remember." Skeeter reassured Ham with a smile of her own.

With one last nod of his head, the big squirrel climbed the tree slowly but surely, his fluffy tail bobbing back and forth. Jay took that as his cue and headed down the trunk in the other direction. Skeeter followed Jay, reassuring herself that the chipmunk was fully capable of getting her back to where they first met.

About a foot from the bottom of the tree, Jay jumped and seemed to float through the air like a kite, softly landing on the ground on all fours. Skeeter, not wanting to be shown up, leapt from

The Case of the Curious Rat

the tree a bit higher up, then added a twist just before hitting the ground. She didn't land as nicely as her friend had, but was rewarded with an open-mouthed look of approval by the chipmunk.

"Ready when you are," Skeeter said just to rub it in. Jay's whiskers twitched one more time before he smiled, turned swiftly, then ran off into the underbrush.

Jay kept the pace slow and even so Skeeter had a chance to take in the beautiful sights of the surrounding woods. The view was spectacular from the top of "The Log," but the forest floor just looked like a green carpet the day before since Skeeter was in pain and anxious about nearly being killed. She was too numb to notice the details of her surroundings then. Now that she was down on forest floor and not in pain, Skeeter could the diverse plant life that overflowed in the woods. Wild flowers of various colors, shapes, and sizes grew alongside tufts of green grass that were as tall and tangled as a bush, to close-cropped and shorter than the flowers growing around them.

The woods were also alive with other animals. Jay and Skeeter laughed out loud as they ran back and forth through the woods. Squirrels of many different sizes and colors ran up and down surrounding trees. Families of chipmunks scurried out from under the bushes. Even a mole poked his head out of his hole to see what the commotion was about, and Skeeter had to quickly leap over him so they wouldn't have a head-on collision. He yelled something at her in anger but she was already too far away to hear him.

It felt good to run freely through the woods again as the wind blew Skeeter's fur back while the sun beat down through the trees in small warm circles. She would definitely miss the magic of these woods, with all the different sights and sounds that she never knew existed, all the animals living together, loving each other and treating each other like family. Skeeter had no idea that it was possible for so many different animals to get along. She lost track of time while gliding through the underbrush behind her new friend, lost in her thoughts.

Skeeter was so distracted that she almost ran into Jay when he came to a sudden stop just inside a low hanging bush. He rose up on his back legs, and then raised his nose to sniff the air. His whiskers twitched and his tail swept back and forth nervously.

"What's wrong?" Skeeter noticed Jay's concern.

"Thought I heard something," was all he said.

"Heard what?" Skeeter inched closer to Jay and started to feel more concerned herself.

He didn't answer her, but his ears twitched and his nose sniffed the air again. Skeeter imitated his posture and rose up on her back legs. She didn't smell anything but she knew her nose wasn't as keen as Jay's because he was accustomed to using his animal senses while she'd lived her whole life indoors. Even if she did smell something, she probably wouldn't even know what it was. She had good hearing but couldn't hear anything that might have made Jay nervous.

"Maybe you just heard us," she said as quietly as she could.

"I don't think so. It was faint. I only heard it for a split second, but I'm sure it was there."

"You don't hear it now?" Skeeter looked around briefly.

"No, but we need to be careful from here on

out." Jay pointed off into the woods. "That tree there is where I found you yesterday. There are a lot of predators from this point on, so we need to be extra careful."

Skeeter didn't realize that they had already traveled all the way back to where she met Jay. She scanned the surrounding woods for any sign of trouble. "I don't see anything, so maybe we just…"

"Shhh!" Jay snapped.

Skeeter heard it too, just for an instant –a soft whisper that was barely audible. Jay's and Skeeter's ears flicked forward, almost in unison, to try to catch the sound again. Besides the bugs chirping in the distance and an occasional bird call, there were no other sounds. Jay waited a few moments before he spoke again, a lot softer this time. "Well, might as well not wait here all day long. Just stay behind me and go where I go. Try not to make too much noise and we should be good."

"Guess the fun is over, huh?" Skeeter gave her companion a small smile.

"Unfortunately," he smiled back, "so just stay with me."

Jay quietly moved forward, always staying under any bush, downed branch or tuft of grass that he could find, always moving as slowly and quietly as possible. Any time they needed to move over a long distance, Jay would go first to chart the path from cover to cover, and signal Skeeter to cross when he thought it was clear. Skeeter moved fast and low to the ground, jumping over anything that might snap under her weight. She also moved in a slightly diagonal direction, crisscrossing like Jay told her to make it harder for predators to catch her.

When Jay and Skeeter stopped for a quick breather beneath large wild flowers that grew into a natural floral cave, they heard the sound again. This time it was louder and more distinguishable. Skeeter got a sick feeling in her stomach.

"That was somebody yelling for help, sounds a little way off still" Jay said.

The soft yell came again and Skeeter knew right away why she had gotten a sick feeling in her stomach. She would recognize that voice anywhere.

"What's wrong?" Jay must have seen the worry

on Skeeter's face.

"I know who that is!" Skeeter bolted off into the direction the yell had come from before waiting for a response from Jay.

"Skeeter, wait! That's the wrong direction!" She heard him yell but didn't pay any attention to him.

Skeeter had never run so hard in her life. Her lungs were on fire from the effort of running at such a breakneck pace. Large blades of grass and low hanging branches slapped against Skeeter's face and sides, leaving small whelps and stinging bruises all over her body. She could hear Thena's voice just ahead, and the yelling was unmistakably Thena's voice even though Skeeter couldn't make out the words. Her friend was in trouble and need help, and that's all that mattered to Skeeter.

She spared a quick glance behind her and saw that Jay was trying to keep up. His shorter legs made it difficult, and he was slowly falling behind. She didn't know how she knew, but somehow Skeeter realized that she couldn't spare even one second to let her new friend catch up. She had to get to her destination as quickly as possible.

Chapter Nine

Ride 'em Cowboy

Thena woke with a start as a shiver ran up her spine. She didn't remember exactly when she fell asleep but it had been sometime after her unwelcome guest stopped talking and moved down the tunnel a short distance. Thena waited patiently, considering the moment she could make her getaway.

She felt the cold seeping into her from being down in the tunnel for such a long period of time without direct sunlight. Her body temperature had to stay above eighty degrees for her to remain comfortable, and right now it was well below that and she could feel it in her bones. Thena needed to get into the sunlight or she was going to freeze to death so she decided to try and make a run for the surface.

Her legs cramped and her whole body felt stiff as she made her way to the opening of the little tunnel. She poked her head out slowly, desperately trying not to make a sound. Light bathed the tunnel floor off to her left. She sighed softly at the prospect of being under sunlight once again. She could only see a short distance into the other direction before total blackness obscured her view. No sounds came from that direction and she couldn't see any movement either.

She quietly lowered her aching body down into the tunnel and slowly made her way towards the sunlight and freedom. The light blinded her at first, leaving large yellow spots in her vision that dissolved so she could see clear daylight skies overhead. She made the short jump to a root hanging out of a wall, and then easily raised herself over the lip of the tunnel's opening into the welcoming sunlight. She instantly felt her leathery skin start to warm up in the heat, but she knew it would take some time for her body to recover from the abusive cold and her hard trek.

The sky above the tunnel was clear, but she realized the tunnel had taken her further into the woods than she thought it would after scanning her surroundings. Thena had no way to determine which way was back towards the house or deeper into the woods, and the situation made her realize that she didn't have any kind of plan at all. She scolded herself for thinking she would just go into the woods and somehow find her friend all on her own.

Thena scanned the surrounding woods for any clues to help her choose the right direction with no success. The woods all looked the same to her, and it was all tall trees covered with bright green leaves, tall bundles of weeds, short round bushes and downed limbs and branches. She could hear the sounds of other animals all around her yet deeper into the trees, but couldn't see any that she might be able to ask for information. If she could find out which direction the houses were in, that would at least narrow down her options a little.

Thena finally made up her mind and picked a direction. Even if it wasn't the right way, Thena knew she couldn't just stand around all day in the same spot. She needed to get going, especially since she still didn't know where the black snake disappeared to once he left her alone. That meant she couldn't even afford to waste time bathing in the sun to get her body temperature up a little higher. Thena kept low to the ground, trying to stay hidden as she moved forward while getting as much direct sunlight as possible. Small circles of sunlight spilled through the trees, so she made sure to spend at least a quick second in each.

Thena froze when she heard the sound of snapping branches off to her left. She could tell that there was something big moving over there, but she couldn't see what it was. She could occasionally make out a brown blur, but it disappeared as quickly as it appeared. Thena was surprised when she realized her beard was out so she quickly relaxed it.

She lost track of time as she continued on her way through the woods as quietly as possible, only stopping long enough to soak up a couple of seconds of direct sunlight. Thena's body was starting to recover from the cold, dark tunnel but she began to feel a little fatigued from not eating in a while. Missing meals wasn't something that Thena was used to and she wasn't going to make a habit of it.

The Case of the Curious Rat

She found a nice big circle of sunlight that had some cover to hide under so she could scout out a nice location to do some hunting. Bugs chirped all around her but she couldn't pin point a specific location to track them down. She longed to be back in her cage or even the flower garden where her prey just muddled around lazily. It would make things so much easier. Thena spotted a tree stump and a large hollowed out log close by that looked promising. She wasn't used to picking a location to hunt but figured either one of those spots could be good.

"Lost yet, little bug?" Thena spun around at the all too recognizable voice behind her. A small smile spread across the black snake's face. "I can sssee by the ssstartled look on your face that you thought I had forgotten about you."

Thena felt frozen from her neck down. Even if she could have gotten her brain to tell the rest of her body to run she doubted it would have listened. The black monster was coiled with its head raised up, eyes piercing. It amazed her that the snake had gotten so close to her without making a sound.

"At leassst make thisss a little fun for me little

bug." It flicked its tongue at her mockingly.

"How…where did you…" Thena couldn't get the rest of the question past her lips.

"I never left you, little bug. It jussst amusssed me to make you think you had gained your freedom." His smile grew bigger. "I have to admit that it wasss wonderful watching you sneak around like you knew what you were doing. Most just run as fast asss they can with no hope of essscape, but you really brought a sssmile to my face. Thank you little bug."

She couldn't believe what a monster her pursuer was, not just in size but in its treatment of other animals. Anger coursed through Thena's body at the thought of others going through what she had gone through.

"You're a monster." Thena barely managed to spit the insult. Her whole body was shaking but she couldn't tell if it was from fear or anger anymore.

"Well, thank you, little bug." The snake was so smug, and Thena wanted to slap that smile right off his face. "I'm afraid our fun is over."

The snake coiled up for its death strike but

Thena was tired of playing the victim. She puffed her beard out as far as she could and yelled. "NEVER!" The snake paused in surprise which gave Thena the valuable seconds she needed to close the distance between them.

Thena flung herself at the serpent with reckless abandon, yelling with wild fury, knowing there was no way she was going to survive this encounter but she didn't care anymore. All she wanted to do was make this predator's life just a little bit harder.

They collided with more force than Thena would have thought possible. Air was knocked from her lungs and her left side briefly went numb. She gathered her wits quickly and swung her thick tail into the side of the snake's head. Her spikes weren't sharp but they had the desired effect. He yelled out in surprise, shaking from the stings to his face. It didn't take him long to recover, and he struck back with lightning quick speed. Thena tried to side-step from his grasp but he still grabbed her by the base of the tail. She screamed out in pain as he tossed her a good distance into the old tree stump. Black beetles scurried away, tittering mockingly at the sudden impact.

Thena felt dizzy and her back hurt when she flipped back onto her feet. Her attacker gave her no time to recover. He slithered forward surprisingly fast for such a large animal. Thena had never seen anything like it and was sure she never would again.

The snake struck several more times, but Thena managed to just barely get out of the way each time. His yellow then red eyes flashed in anger with every failed attempt.

"Thisss isss getting boring little bug," the snake hissed with its black lips parted in a growl.

"THEN END IT IF YOU CAN!" Thena yelled back angrily at the snake. "But I'll not be an easy meal, I promise you that!"

"All meals are easy," the snake replied before he laughed at her. "Some just take longer to get down, but you'll still be a meal in the end."

"Bring it, then!" Thena yelled in anger, then lowered herself to the ground and shifted her weight to her back legs in anticipation.

Thena's instincts paid off and she was ready for the snake when he struck. Instead of jumping clear out of his way when he struck this time, she sidestepped and left him striking at empty air. She immediately jumped on him and bit down as hard as she could right behind his head. Thena didn't have teeth but the snake still grunted in pain as her jaw clamped down on his thick body. She hung on for dear life as he tried to shake her free, and she knew she needed to keep her grip on him so he couldn't get another opportunity to strike. She knew that sooner or later either he would tire out or her grip would slip and it would be the end of their little fight.

Finally, the monster got tired of shaking Thena and decided to try a different tactic. He slammed his body against the ground as hard as he could, and landed right on top of her. The blow knocked the air out of her lungs and sent a tingling sensation up her backbone. Her jaws instantly released as he slithered across her. She needed to get a hold on him again so he couldn't get enough distance between them to line up for another strike. She felt pain in her back end before she even knew what was happening. She twisted her body so that she was bent in half and saw that the black snake had gotten a grip on her. The pain was intense as it climbed her hind legs and back. Her eyes watered from the pain. She instantly started clawing at his face and eyes get him to let go, but her needle thin claws barely scratched his black scales.

Thena yelled out for help as she continued clawing, not that she expected anyone to answer her last minute pleas. Jaws tightened around her, doubling the pain going up her body. The pain made Thena wonder how much more she could take before blacking out. She doubled her yelling efforts and increased her clawing, though neither had any effect on her attacker.

To her surprise, she was again tossed against the old tree stump. This time she hit it with enough force that the wood splintered and rained down on her. Dust filled her nose and eyes. Thena tried to get back to her feet but it hurt too much. Her head was throbbing and she could barely see through the tears and dust.

Thena lay down on the soft grass, knowing this was the end. A large circle of light broke through the trees and bathed her in its warmth. It made her think of home and Skeeter. She just hopped that somehow, even in the middle of all this chaos, Skeeter was ok and would be able to find her way home. Tears filled her eyes again thinking about her friend and the short time they had spent together. All the talks they had, even if she just wanted to be left alone. Thena regretted not telling Skeeter that she was a true friend.

"It's good to sssee that you finally realize the hopelessness of fighting." She hated that this bully thought she was giving up and tried to rise to her feet again, but she suffered shooting pains that knocked her back to the ground.

"Just get it over with," she snarled.

Her attacker smiled at her. "If that isss what you wish," he snarled back.

The black snake rose up to strike, but instead of coming at Thena he pitched sideways and yelled in pain. At first she thought the snake had gone crazy, rolling around and writhing on the ground, but then she noticed something clamped on the back of it, at the base of its head. She tried to clear the dust and tears from her eyes again by blinking but it didn't work. Had something struck the snake or had someone come to her aid?

Her vision finally cleared enough to make out another object hit the snake. This time, it pitched forward with the weight of the two objects. Its long black body curled up into a knotted mass and the two objects disappeared under the black mass. Thena was shocked to realize she actually had two rescuers. She rose to her feet again with renewed vigor. Her legs and back screamed in agony, but she ignored it and readied herself to rejoin the fight. Before she could take another step, the snake unraveled itself in a flurry and the two figures landed on their feet not far from where she stood.

Thena had to do a double take when she saw Skeeter standing alongside a strange chipmunk.

"Skeeter..." she said dumbly.

"Hey Thena," Skeeter smiled, "sounded like you could use some help."

"Oh, you bet I could!" Thena wanted to run over to her friend and give her the biggest hug ever, but the black snake was gathering himself for another attack.

As her attacker slithered closer, Thena noticed that one of its red eyes was now closed with a nasty looking cut on it. Either Skeeter or her companion had delivered a well-placed scratch.

"Well, well. Now isn't thisss a pleasant

sssurprise?" The snake licked its lips mockingly. "Now I have dinner and dessert, and rat just happens to be my favorite." Anger seemed to radiate from the black monster, as a ripple of excitement seemed to run down his black scales. "You'll pay for doing this to my eye, little one."

"Just leave us alone and no one else needs to get hurt," said Skeeter.

"Let's just run for it," whispered the chipmunk.

"Oh, yesss! Make a run for it!" The snake taunted the trio. "That will be so much fun!"

Skeeter shook her head at the chipmunk. "I don't think we could outrun him, besides Thena doesn't even look like she could keep up."

Thena was glad Skeeter had said it because she didn't want to admit it out loud that she was in worse shape than she looked. "I agree. If we run, he'll just pick us off one at a time."

"Ok," said the chipmunk. "I'll stay with you guys."

The snake didn't look happy with the decision they made. Thena could almost feel the anger and heat coming from the snake. His skin rippled and shone like glass in the sunlight. For the first time Thena started to feel hopeful about her situation. She knew that they couldn't possibly beat the huge snake, but maybe they could inconvenience it enough that it would give up and try to find an easier meal.

The predator looked like he was done talking; the determination on his face was evident as he gathered up for another strike. He was through playing games and Thena could clearly see it on his face.

"Now, what do we have here," a voice boomed. Thena was shocked when the biggest squirrel she had ever seen came marching out of the woods between where she and Skeeter stood. "Are you bullying animals smaller than you again?"

Thena couldn't believe the big squirrel talked that way and the snake just stood there blinking at him.

"This isss no concern of yoursss Ham," it hissed at the squirrel.

"Ah, but it isss," Ham hissed back mockingly. "You see, this rat has the protection of The Log, so that protection extends to the lizard as well considering that they're friends, I believe." Skeeter nodded her assurance at the squirrel.

"Wait, Skeeter, you know him?" Thena felt lost. How had Skeeter found the time to make friends?

"Oh, yeah. Me and Ham go way back," Skeeter smiled at Thena.

"Oh, yeah. Way back." Ham's deep voice still surprised Thena.

"Your protection doesn't extend thisss far from the log, Ham. You know that." The snake was insistent.

"This time, I think we can make an exception." Ham's voice almost sounded like a growl.

The snake seemed to be a bit subdued for the moment, so Thena finally allowed herself to relax a little. She stretched her legs trying to get them back into working order and let her beard relax. Her whole body cramped and her face felt swollen. She could only imagine what she looked like, all swollen and covered in dust.

"You just think you can protect every pest in these woods, right Ham? How dare you presume to interfere with me!" The snake was indignant.

"Then find some different woods to hunt in, Tiny," Ham said.

"Don't you call me that!" The snake spit angrily.

"Oh, I'm sorry. I forgot that you don't like to be called Tiny."

Thena heard snickering and looked over to find Skeeter and her companion quietly laughing and whispering to each other. Ham joined them but his laughs boomed through the clearing.

"Ham, wait. Is his name really Tiny?" Skeeter couldn't believe it.

"You see, when Tiny was just a little guy, his mom was top predator of these woods. She was a vicious hunter but not a bully like our Tiny here." Ham kept his eyes on Tiny the entire time he spoke to make sure he didn't make any sudden movements. "Anyway, Tiny used to love to go off exploring without telling his mom where he was going, so she would wander the woods yelling 'TINY!' Of course, no one ever forgot mommy's little nickname when she passed and Tiny here took over as head predator."

"You're gonna pay for…" Tiny hissed.

"Let's stay calm, Tiny…" Ham interrupted the hissing snake.

Thena couldn't help herself. She joined the others in laughing at the big snake. Skeeter rolled on the ground laughing so hard she sounded like she couldn't catch her breath.

"STOP CALLING ME TINY!" The snake's yell echoed through the forest and he slithered forward lighting quick.

Before Tiny could get close enough to strike, a second squirrel sprinted out from under a nearby bush and hit Tiny on the back. This squirrel was half as big as Ham and it looked like his tail had gotten caught in something that had pulled most of the fur out.

Instead of biting or clawing the snake, he slipped a piece of string around his head like a leash. Tiny instantly started bucking up and down to try and get the scrawny squirrel off its back with no luck. The squirrel held the string in an iron grip with one paw and waved the other over his head yelling "YEEEHAW" the entire time. He looked like one of the cowboys she had seen on Max's TV.

Thena couldn't help herself. She started

cheering on the squirrel with delight and soon everybody was cheering with her. They cheered him on as he waved his free hand about, whooping and hollering. Thena wouldn't have believed it if she hadn't seen it herself.

Tiny finally decided that all this aggravation wasn't worth it, and he slithered off into the woods, defeated.

The skinny squirrel jumped clear of the snake as it disappeared under some brush and scampered over to where the rest of them had come together. He had the biggest smile on his face that Thena had ever seen.

"Nice job, Bean," the chipmunk said.

"That was the most fun I've had in a long time Jay! Isn't that right Ham, most fun in a long time? We should hang with Jay more often, don't you think?"

Thena was amazed at how fast the skinny squirrel could talk.

"That sounds like a good idea, Bean," Ham said.

Thena was introduced to all of Skeeter's new

friends and they welcomed her warmly to the woods saying, "Any friend of Skeeter's is a friend of ours."

"Guys, I don't want to break up the celebration but we should get some place safe." Jay was always the voice of reason.

"Right, Jay. You said you knew a place. Is it big enough for all of us?" Ham asked.

"Yup, should do nicely and we should be able to get there before the sun goes down if we hurry."

"Okay, let's stay together then. I'll help Thena." The big squirrel smiled at her. "Wanna go for a ride, little missy?"

Thena's whole body still hurt and her face felt swollen, but she got on Ham's back with Bean's help. Jay took the lead with Skeeter by his side. The two brothers stayed close behind them with their longer legs. Thena's pride hurt more than anything because she was reduced to riding on the squirrels back, but she would have been left behind a long time ago at the pace they were moving. After a while, she actually started to feel nice and comfortable snuggled in the squirrel's fur, but she wasn't about to tell the others that.

The sun was low by the time they got to their destination. Orange and yellow rays of sunlight peeked from behind distant hills. The tree Jay stopped in front of was at the edge of the woods but nowhere near anywhere Thena recognized. Concrete structures stuck out of the ground and looked like the beginnings of houses, but Thena could never be sure about the things humans did. Big yellow machinery was parked all around the site, and a flimsy looking orange fence surrounded the whole thing.

After some slight jostling and some hanging on by Thena, they made it to the tree branch where Jay said they would stay the night. A large hole big enough for everyone but Ham went deep into the trunk, but Ham said he would rather sleep outside during the night to guard the opening.

Thena finally allowed herself to relax after she crawled through the tunnel. Jay had been right; there was plenty of room inside. However, Bean decided to sleep outside with his brother, so Thena was alone inside with Skeeter and Jay. Thena smiled the biggest smile she could manage when the two started talking at the same time. They asked her how she felt, if she was hungry, and even questions about her trek into the woods.

"What are you smiling about?" Skeeter wondered what Thena found so amusing.

"Just glad to hear your voice again, Skeeter. You can't imagine how much I've missed you." Thena smiled again at her best friend.

"I've missed you, too," Skeeter smiled back. "Just get some rest and we'll talk more on the way home tomorrow. I'm sure Ham and Bean will help us get home safe and sound."

The thought of getting home made Thena smile again. "Sounds good to me."

Thena fell asleep listening to Jay and Skeeter talking softly about Tiny the snake. She would have to tell Skeeter all about the adventure she had been on and it didn't bother her one bit. She was reunited with Skeeter again. Skeeter was her best friend in the whole world, besides Max, and Thena was never gonna let her best friend out of her sight ever again. Tomorrow they would start another adventure: the adventure home!

Acknowledgments

This book is dedicated to my family's best friends, Thena and Skeeter. I wasn't so sure about having a bearded dragon and a rat as pets for the kids, but they turned out to be the funniest and best pets we have ever had. Thank you Thena and Skeeter for all the laughs and good times. We will never forget you.

Thank you also to my family, and especially my kids, who support everything I do, no matter what. Thank you for laughing at all my jokes and for listening to all the "useless information" I talk about. You guys are my rock and my lifeline when I am adrift. I'm glad Thena and Skeeter snuck into the house so that I would be inspired to write their story.